Six Under th

6 six ⠿

Bruce T. Lindley Public School

The children made a **big** picture of the sea.

They made six little fish.
One, two, three,
four, five, six little fish.

The children made six big fish.

One blue fish,

two green fish,

and three yellow fish.

The big fish
will swim after the little fish.

The children made six brown rocks.

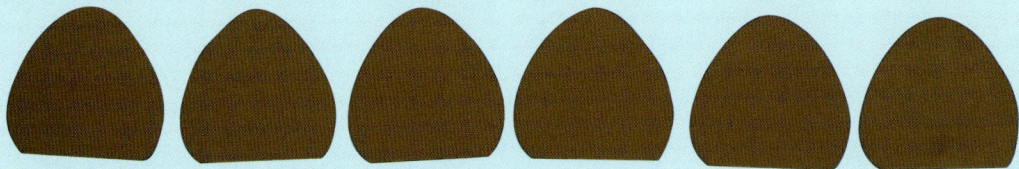

They put the six brown rocks in a line.

The children made six red crabs.

They put the crabs on the rocks.

The children made six white shells.
They made three little shells
and three big shells.

They put the shells by the rocks.

The children made six tiny sea horses.

The sea horses went ...

up and down,

       up and down,

              up and down.

Can you count ...

six little fish,

six big fish,

six brown rocks,

six red crabs,

six white shells,

six tiny sea horses?

Under the Sea

6 little fish

6 big fish

6 brown rocks

6 white shells

6 red crabs

6 tiny sea horses

16